How to Survive (and perhaps thrive)
On a Teacher's Salary

How to Survive (and perhaps thrive) On a Teacher's Salary

Danny Kofke

Tate Publishing & Enterprises

TATE PUBLISHING
& *Enterprises*

Tate Publishing is committed to excellence in the publishing industry. Our staff of highly trained professionals, including editors, graphic designers, and marketing personnel, work together to produce the very finest books available. The company reflects the philosophy established by the founders, based on Psalms 68:11,

"THE LORD GAVE THE WORD AND GREAT WAS THE COMPANY OF THOSE WHO PUBLISHED IT."

If you would like further information, please contact us:
1.888.361.9473 | www.tatepublishing.com
TATE PUBLISHING & *Enterprises*, LLC | 127 E. Trade Center Terrace
Mustang, Oklahoma 73064 USA

Published in the United States of America

ISBN: 978-1-5988690-2-6

07.06.02

This book is dedicated to all you teachers out there.
Thank you for making the world a better place.

Acknowledgments

I must begin by thanking my beautiful wife, Tracy. You are not only my wife, but my best friend as well. Thanks for sacrificing so much to help us reach our goals.

To my wonderful daughter, Ava. Thank you for bringing great joy into my life. You are the best daughter a father could hope to have.

Mom, Dad, Meno and Art; thank you for the valuable lessons you have taught me. You were, and continue to be, great role models. Thank you for everything

Thank you to all the wonderful people at Tate Publishing. Your hard work helped make one of my dreams become reality.

To the rest of my family and friends, thank you for all of your love and support.

Table of Contents

Introduction

I guess you could say that I have always been somewhat frugal with money. My mother likes to tell the story of when I was younger and the family would play card games together. My mom, dad, brother and I would put pennies in the pot and play for them. She remembers how competitive I was to win these pennies so I could put them in my piggy bank.

I knew I wanted to become a teacher after having Mr. Stutzke as my civics teacher in 9th grade. He was an amazing person and educator. I know you might be thinking, "You like money and wanted to be a teacher?" Not a good mix, huh? Well, throughout college I worked various jobs making minimum wage. I lived at home most of this time so I was able to save a little money even though I only made an average of $5.00 an hour. As a college student I remember thinking, "I can't wait to graduate so I can become a teacher and make a lot of money." I guess when you make minimum wage, $30,000 a year sounds like a lot.

Although this book was written with teachers in mind, I believe the practices taught can benefit anyone, from firefighters and policemen, to CEO's and business owners. In this book, I will show you how my wife and I were able to visit ten foreign countries, pay-off a brand new car in two years, and even have one of us stay home for the first year of my daughter's life—all on a teacher's salary! Do I have your attention yet? If so, let's go and I'll show you how it can be done.

Chapter 1

LAYING THE FOUNDATION

Before I begin, I must tell you that I was blessed with some good fortune, but along the way I took some risks and worked hard. I began working when I was fourteen years old. My family owned an appliance business and I delivered and set-up appliances during my summer break. My motivation to work, at this time, was a car. My parents agreed to match the amount I earned. Instead of hanging out with my friends all summer, I lifted heavy appliances in the hot Florida sun. I continued to do this in the afternoons once school started. By the time I turned sixteen, I had saved $2,000! With my parents matching this amount, I had enough to buy a $4,000 car. My grandfather was looking to purchase a new vehicle and was kind enough to sell me his truck for the amount I had. This was my first real understanding of money. I realized that if I worked hard and saved, I could buy something that I desired.

I was fortunate that my parents gave me money, but even more fortunate that they made me work to earn this amount. Some of my friends had their cars and other items bought for them by their parents and, let me tell you, they did not treat their possessions like I did mine. I valued what I had because I knew how much sweat went into earning it. Think about some of your possessions. Which ones do you value more—the ones you worked for or the ones that were given to you? I bet many of you said the ones you worked for. My parents helped teach me a valuable lesson by making me work for the things I desired.

Even though I worked, I still managed to do well in school (I usually made the A/B honor roll) and even played on my high school baseball team. During the fall, I continued to deliver appliances and was a valet at a local country club. I saved the money I earned from these jobs to pay for my expenses during baseball season when I could not work because I was busy with practices and games.

As I mentioned earlier, I lived with my parents most of my college life. My first two years of college, spent at a local community college, were paid for by an academic scholarship (see, you can work and still earn good grades). My last two years of college were paid for by my grandmother. Now some of you might be thinking, "Well, that's nice for you Danny, but we did not have a kind and loving person pay for our college expenses so we had to get a student loan." I was very fortunate that I did have my college paid for, BUT I still continued to work this entire time to pay for my everyday expenses. I know some people do not work during their college years and, thus, have to borrow more money with their student loans. This increases the amount they will have to eventually pay back—along with the added interest. If you are currently in school using a loan to pay for your education, I strongly encourage you to use this loan to pay for your educational expenses only.

At my college, the final semester for an elementary education major was spent student teaching—without getting paid! This meant that I went from August until the end of November working for free. Knowing this, I spent the previous summer working full time at a golf course and saved as much as I could. When August rolled around, I had a few thousand dollars in the bank to get me through this time. I know it may sound like I did nothing during my college years except go to class and work, but I did manage to go out and have fun too—I was just responsible about it and knew how much money I was able to spend.

I will never forget August 9th, 1999. This was the first teacher workday of my student teaching semester and, more importantly, the day I met the love of my life, Tracy. I was assigned to student teach in Mrs. Cindy Rodriguez's first grade classroom. Tracy was a fellow first grade teacher and I remember thinking at the end of the day that she would become my wife—who says there is not love at first sight?

During the start of my internship, I continued to work at the golf course on Saturdays to earn a little spending money. This did not last very long because I was running myself ragged working six days a week. I hated leaving this job because it provided me money for going out to dinner and other social activities, but I didn't want to burn myself out before I even began my career.

As the months passed, Tracy and I grew closer and closer until I decided that it was time to pop the question. There was only one slight problem—how was I going to pay for the engagement ring? This was solved by what my family refers to as the Bank of Meno. Meno is my wonderful grandmother who paid for the majority of my college expenses. She loved Tracy too, so she gladly agreed to lend me $1,800 so I could buy the ring. I proposed in December, Tracy said yes, and then we had to prepare for another expense—*the wedding!*

Upon graduating in December, I began to substitute teach. Using the practices that had served me so well up until this time, I saved some of the money I earned teaching and gave the rest to Meno to pay off the engagement ring loan. I can proudly state that this loan was paid off by February.

Around this time, Tracy and I decided to look into the possibility of teaching overseas. A friend of ours had told us about some people she knew who taught internationally and absolutely loved it. We decided to research this possibility to see if it was something we wanted to pursue.

Our first step was to find out how we could apply to teach overseas. We decided to go through a company called International Schools Services. In order to use this company, a teacher must possess a minimum of a four-year bachelor's degree and have at least two years of full-time teaching experience. I thought we could not go through this company because I did not have any teaching experience, but ISS encourages teaching teams to apply, so Tracy and I could go in together as a team.

We then had to each pay $175 and complete two narratives. The first narrative asked us to write a statement describing the personal and professional qualifications and experiences we had that would enable us to be successful in an international school. The second narrative asked us to tell what made us outstanding educators. Both of these narratives were to be between 200–400 words in length. Tracy and I completed these, sent in our money, and waited to hear if we had been accepted.

We received word in late December that we had been accepted and made plans to attend the hiring fair scheduled for mid-February in Boston, Massachusetts. We went up there with open minds and had no clue what to expect.

We were overwhelmed upon arriving at the job fair. There were schools from over 200 countries represented— schools from Afghanistan to Zimbabwe. Luckily for us, a few directors (principals) had read our resumes and wanted to interview us. We interviewed for positions at schools in Nigeria, Bahrain, and Poland. The school in Bahrain offered us a job right after our interview. We asked if we could have an hour to talk about it. We went with our gut feelings and decided to turn down these jobs. The director of this school seemed pushy and something told us that this was not the place for us. It was hard to turn down a job and hope we would get offered another one. This weekend had cost us around $1,000 and we might have had to leave Boston without jobs and, thus, waste this money, but we had to do what felt right.

We interviewed for the school in Nigeria next and thought it went well. Our last interview was for a school in Krakow, Poland. After this interview, we walked around Boston trying to clear our minds. As you can imagine, this was a very stressful weekend and we needed some fresh air.

The next day, which was a Saturday, we got a call in the afternoon from Melissa, the director of the school in Poland, telling us to come back to her room in one hour for a follow-up interview. This interview went well. At the conclusion, Melissa told us that she would be calling us the following day, before we left Boston, to let us know if we got the jobs.

On Sunday we sat around our room waiting to hear from Melissa. After waiting a few hours, we decided to get out because we were going out of our minds. We returned to the hotel in the afternoon to check-out. Melissa had left a message with the front desk saying, "Have a safe trip home and I'll call you there." Aaahh! We flew home that night still not knowing if we were going to teach overseas.

Melissa finally called the following day and told us that the American International School of Krakow had hired us. We were relieved, excited, and nervous at the same time. I would be teaching a kindergarten/first grade class and Tracy a second/third/fourth grade class. Although we did not know it at the time, this experience would lay the foundation for our financial success. If international teaching sounds appealing to you, please visit the International Schools Services website at www.iss.edu for more information.

Okay, time for a quick recap. Tracy and I met in August, got engaged in December, accepted jobs in Poland in February, and were getting married in June. It was quite a busy year, if I do say so myself. Now came the fun and stressful part—planning and paying for a wedding. We talked about the type of wedding we wanted and decided to go all out. I know that does not sound like me, but I figured you only get married once (hopefully) and I wanted it to be a special day. We added all the expenses and they came to approximately $10,000.

Now the big question—How in the world were we going to come up with $10,000? If you said, "What is the Bank of Meno," then you are correct. Once again I was lucky enough to borrow money, interest free. I know there are many people who have extravagant weddings and spend tons of money that they do not have on them. I understand that a wedding day is special and unforgettable, but it is only one day. By going into debt before even starting their lives together, couples can actually sabotage their marriages because when the bills start coming in, the arguing and stress begins. Tracy and I knew that moving to Poland would provide us a way to borrow $10,000 for our wedding (I will tell you how in the next chapter) and pay it back in a short period of time.

Chapter 2

THE BEGINNING OF FINANCIAL FREEDOM

Tracy and I left Florida in August of 2000 to embark on our exciting adventure. It was very risky leaving our comfort zones, but you know how the saying goes, "Nothing ventured, nothing gained." It was hard adjusting to our new lives in Poland. The little things we took for granted were now somewhat difficult. It was a challenge to even buy a banana at first, but after a few months, we became more acclimated to our new surroundings.

There were many great things about teaching and living in Poland. These included small class sizes, well-behaved students, the chance to travel, and the opportunity to save money. Our salaries were close to what we earned in the States except for one difference—we did not have to pay taxes. During the years we taught in Krakow, Americans were allowed to earn up to $75,000 a year overseas without having to pay taxes on this money. In addition, our housing was paid for and we did not need a vehicle because we either walked—which was good for our waistlines after eating kielbasa and pierogi—or we took trams wherever we needed to go. One of the biggest advantages in moving to Poland was it enabled us to pay off the Bank of Meno. Since we knew that we were going to be living primarily in Poland for two years, we decided to sell our cars. We used this money to pay off our wedding. We were on our way to living comfortably on teacher salaries.

Budgeting

I know a lot of people don't like this word because it sounds too restrictive. As most of us know, if someone says you can't have something, you want it even more. This is the reason that most diets fail. As soon as you are not allowed to eat a certain food, you crave it until you give in to your urges and end up eating more than you normally would have. This holds true with budgeting as well. Let's say you want a new, high-definition television set to watch movies and your favorite team on. The t.v. costs more than your budget allows, but you know a way you can get it in time for the Super Bowl—*charge it!* You end up putting this purchase on a credit card and thus ensure the credit card company of making a nice little profit after you pay off your bill with a lot of interest added to the original price of the t.v. Not a smart move if you ask me. I have a better way of getting this television.

Be Like Mike, Er. . . . David

The David who you should be like is David Bach, an author who has written numerous books that I highly recommend you read. Mr. Bach explains in great detail a sure fire way of saving money. It is a concept known as Pay Yourself First. Using this method, you can purchase almost anything your heart desires without having those ugly interest payments. If this sounds like a good plan to you, keep reading and see how it works.

We are going to use the before-mentioned television. For this example, we are going to put the cost of this t.v. at $2,000. Upon receiving your paycheck, put away a set amount of money before you spend any of it. If you want the television in one year, set aside $165 a month. If you want it in six months, pay yourself $330 each month. Now you might say, "Danny, I work hard, have kids, a mortgage, two car payments and I want to reward myself for working so hard." I could not agree more. I just want you to do this sensibly. If you pay yourself first, you might not have enough money left over to eat out every weekend or go to the movies once a week. Just think how sweet it will be to watch your favorite show knowing that you own the television set it is playing on. For more examples, please refer to Mr. Bach's books listed in the bibliography.

I know there are some of you out there that would love to use this philosophy but know you cannot. I am going to show you a way that will enable you to still purchase that television (or whatever else it is that you want) and not pay a lot of interest. Let's stay with the $2,000 amount. If you buy $2,000 worth of items on a credit card that has an 18% interest rate (which is like working five days a week and only getting paid for four, I might add) with a minimum payment of 2% of the balance, your monthly payments will be $40.00. Not too bad, huh? Well, what if I told you that if you made these minimum monthly payments it would take you 370 months to pay this balance off—that is more than thirty years! In addition, the final cost of this $2,000 purchase would be $6,931.15. You would pay almost two and half times the original purchase price in interest only. No wonder you receive all of those credit card brochures in the mail. What a great way for these companies to become wealthy. Later on, I will show how this same concept can help you make money. You are probably thinking, "Now Danny, you just said that you will show me a way to still buy something on credit and not pay much interest. $4,931.15 sounds like a lot of money to me." It does to me, too. How about if you just paid an extra $10 a month towards this loan? How long do you think it would take to pay it off? If you said 62 months, you are the winner. In fact, your total payment for this purchase would be $3,077.25. Just by adding a measly $10 a month to your minimum payment (that's about 33 cents a day), you will pay off this loan more than 25 years earlier and save almost $4,000! Let's say you double the minimum payment and pay $80 each month. Well, your debt would be paid off in less than three years and the total amount spent would be $2,525.59. Although saving for and buying something outright is much more cost efficient than using credit, I have shown you how you can use your credit card and save money.

A few of you might be thinking, "What about those great deals that offer no interest for three years? How can I go wrong with one of these plans? Let me tell you a secret about these "deals." As an example, you buy some nice furniture for your living room that costs $5,000. Let's say the interest rate is 20%, but you do not have to pay this interest for three years. You think you will have this loan, or most of it, paid off by then. You do a great job making monthly payments and after three years the balance of this loan is $1,000. You now think, "Great, I only owe $1,000 with 20% interest added to this." Well, I hate to be the bearer of bad news, but you are wrong. You have to pay 20% interest on the original purchase price—yep, $5,000. So, you go from owing $1,200 (20% added to the $1,000 balance) to owing $2,000 (20% of $5,000 added to the $1,000 balance). No wonder you see these types of plans offered all the time. If you still feel the need to use one of these plans, I hope you now understand the importance of paying off your loan before the interest-free period expires.

Chapter 3

PRACTICE WHAT YOU PREACH—
OUR EUROPEAN EXPERIENCE

Upon arriving in Poland, Tracy and I decided how much money we wanted to have when we returned to the States. Now a lot of people do not plan ahead, and thus, wind up living paycheck to paycheck. We knew that we would be moving back home in two years and decided that $20,000 was a good amount to start with. We divided $20,000 by 24 (the number of months we would earn a salary teaching in Poland) and came up with $834. We then set up a plan with the secretary at our school to deposit this amount into our savings account every time we got paid at the end of each month. By doing this from the beginning of our employment, we never missed that money because we never saw it. Using this approach, we lived off the money deposited into our checking accounts and almost forgot about the money being put into our savings. I feel that this is an important thing to do. If Tracy and I had not put away that money from the beginning, we might have spent it each month because we could have done what many people do today— spend as much as they earn. There are some people who would spend their entire paychecks no matter how much they earn—whether it be $10,000 or $100,000. By automatically putting money away before you see it, you eliminate this problem.

Another important lesson we learned in Poland was developing an idea of how much money we needed each week and spending just that amount. After a few months of getting acclimated to our lives overseas, we began to write down every dollar (or zloty as it was called in Poland) we spent for one month. We then broke this down week by week to see how we spent our money and determined how much we really needed each week. We came up with $200 a week. For some of you this amount could be less, for others more (although I bet if you look at what you spend some of your money on, you will see how you could live off less). The point is to come up with an amount that will enable you to buy your necessities (groceries, gas, etc.) for the week along with a little extra left over to spend how you please. As I mentioned earlier, this figure was $200 for us. Every Friday night I would go to the ATM and get out our $200 for the week. I would usually carry some of it around with me and place the rest in a jar in our apartment (envelopes work well, too). If we ran out of money on Wednesday, we could not buy anything until the end of the week. I know this might sound extreme, but if you are serious about saving money, this is an important step. I know this may sound like the dreaded b-word—budget. I don't look at it that way because if you only have $200 a week to spend and you spend it, you will not have any money left so what is there to budget? Like I mentioned earlier, this practice might sound crazy and far-fetched, but don't knock it until you try it. You might have to tinker with your weekly amount a few times, but I promise you if you use this approach, you will be less careless about how you spend your hard-earned money.

Yes, You Can Save and Still Have Fun

Okay, I know some of you are probably thinking, "Wow Danny, you spent two years in Europe and just saved your money." You are somewhat correct in this response. We did save money, BUT we also traveled, ate out a few nights a week, and bought many neat trinkets. We were lucky that the cost of living in Poland was very low. This helped keep our weekly expenses down. Since we had set up a way to return to America with a nice amount of money and had established a weekly "budget," we decided to use the rest of our salaries on traveling and fun. We knew that we would probably never again have the opportunity to visit so many places, so we took advantage of our situation.

In October 2000, we spent a long weekend in Prague, Czech Republic. In November, it was off for a five-day vacation to Nice, France. We decided to fly home in December to spend Christmas with our families.

The year 2001 saw us in many exotic places. In February, we spent a week in Tunisia, Africa. In April, we traveled to Venice and Florence, Italy for our belated honeymoon.

In June, we spent one week in Seville, Spain and then took a train to Costa del Sol for a week of fun with my family. We all then flew back to Krakow so they could spend some time exploring our wonderful city. In April of 2001, Tracy's sister, Cindy, gave birth to a beautiful baby girl named Aubrey. After she was born, the doctors discovered that she had Cystic Fibrosis (please refer to the appendix for an explanation of this disease). Tracy and I had planned on going to Greece that summer, but after hearing about Aubrey, we decided to fly to Orlando to meet our new niece. After spending one month in Florida, we returned to Krakow to prepare for another year of teaching and traveling. In September, we went back to Prague for a long weekend of shopping. October saw us in Paris for a four-day trip. At the beginning of November, we spent four nights in Berlin, Germany. The week before Thanksgiving found us exploring The Hague, Netherlands. We decided to stay in Europe for Christmas and went to Vienna, Austria for a week. A pretty busy year, huh?

The year 2002 was filled with travel and adventure too. In January, we went on a school field trip to the mountainous town of Zakopane in southern Poland for a ski trip. We spent our winter break in Budapest, Hungary. Around Easter, Tracy's mother and grandmother flew over for a visit. We ventured back to Vienna for five days and then spent the rest of their trip in Poland. By the time we returned to America in June, we had visited a grand total of ten countries and still saved over $20,000! See, I told you that it is possible to save money and still have fun. It takes time and sacrifice, but it can be done.

Chapter 4

MOVING HOME

Tracy and I left Poland in June to embark on our new lives in America. A few months before leaving Krakow, we sat down and re-visited the goals we had set upon arriving in Poland to see if we had accomplished them (which I can gladly say we did). We then began discussing our goals for the future. I feel it is very important to set goals—both short and long-term ones- and sit down every so often and see if you have met these goals or are on the right track to meeting them.

We decided that we would both work for one full year and then start trying to have a baby. This plan would have us both working for almost two years before the baby arrived. We both decided that Tracy would stay home for as long as possible after we had our child.

Sacrifice

In order for us to reach our goal of having Tracy stay home, we knew that we would have to careful with our financial decisions because living off one teacher's salary for a family of three would be difficult. We began the process of meeting this goal as soon as we stepped off the plane in America. We decided to fly into Cleveland, Ohio to spend some time with Tracy's grandparents before heading to Florida to find a house, job, and all the other responsibilities that come with these. We were going to rent a car and drive to Florida after we were done visiting in Ohio, but then we thought, "Why not buy a car here, instead of waiting until we get to Florida, and save the money that would be used towards the rental car?" We only ended up saving around $500 by doing this, but every little bit counts. We bought a brand new Ford Escape. I would not recommend buying a new car, but Tracy's father worked at a Ford dealership and family members of Ford employees got a discount on new cars, so this made it worth the price. We then headed towards Florida in our new car, anxious to begin another chapter in our lives.

The Sacrifice Continues

After arriving in Florida, we began the fun, and often times stressful, task of buying a house. We went into this process expecting to buy a three bedroom, two bathroom home. We then found a two bedroom house that was less expensive than bigger homes. Tracy and I discussed whether we should just go ahead and buy the two bedroom house rather than a bigger and more expensive home. Our main goal at this point in our lives was to have enough money saved so Tracy could stay home in a couple of years. We came to the conclusion that buying this house would keep us on the path to attaining our goal and closed on it two weeks later. I know some of you are probably asking how a family can live in a two bedroom house. Living in Poland helped us realize how little space we really need. We had a one bedroom apartment and never felt cramped. Let's face it, when most people buy bigger houses, they end up accumulating more "stuff" and fill their space with it. How much of this "stuff" is really necessary? I would venture to say not much, but since you have the space, you fill it.

At this time we had another fortunate break. My grand-mother gave us $15,000 to use in purchasing our house. Instead of using that money to buy "stuff" for our home, we applied it to the down payment. We put 20% down, which eliminated us from having to pay mortgage insurance. This ended up saving us thousands of dollars over the course of the loan. I know that we had a nice break in getting this $15,000, but we used this break to our advantage. We could have gone out and bought really expensive furniture and other items to fill our home, but this would not have helped us reach our goals. By putting this money towards our down payment, we greatly reduced our monthly mortgage pay-ments and, thus, made staying home in the future much more attainable.

I know most people do not have the same circumstances that we did. You really want to buy a house, but know there is no way you can save enough to have a down payment. Well, I have good news. If you are a teacher (or a first-time home buyer) there are special programs out there designed just for you! Some mortgage lenders will let you buy a house without putting anything down. With an offer like this, you can definitely purchase your own house and be on the right path to becoming financially secure. If you are a teacher, check out the website, www.homes4teachers.org, to see what type of loans are available to you. You can also shop around at banks in your town to see the types of loans they offer. Another great place to search online is at www.bankrate.com. This site lets you compare rates, has a mortgage calculator so you can see how much money you can afford when buying a house, and offers many other great tools. My main point here is that you should do all you can to buy a house and not rent.

Why Renting Makes You Poor

I know for some of you, renting seems like the only solution, but it is not. As I just explained, many of you can qualify for a loan to purchase a house. Do you know anyone that pays rent for the place he/she lives? If so, do they seem financially secure? I bet not. I am going to show you why most people who rent will never become wealthy.

Let's say you rent a house for $800 a month (this is a pretty low figure, but we will use it as an example) and live there for five years. After five years, you decide it is time to move somewhere else. Guess how much money you will receive upon moving? Zilch, nada, nothing! This means that you have paid $48,000 (60 x $800) and have nothing to show for it. This is not a good way to become financially secure unless you are the one collecting the rent.

In contrast, we are going to say that you bought a house that costs $120,000 and mortgaged it for thirty years at a 7% interest rate. Your monthly payments (excluding insurance and taxes) would be $798.36. You decide to move in five years. Paying almost the same amount as you would renting, you would still owe approximately $113,000 on this house (over $40,000 of your monthly payments would go towards interest). If your home increased in value a modest 3% a year, it would now be worth $139,111. If you sell it for that amount, you will walk away with $26,000 ($139,000-$113,000) to put towards your next home. When you look at it this way, you can clearly see why it makes much more financial sense to buy rather than rent your home.

Cheating the Bank

Speaking of mortgage payments, I want to share a neat little trick concerning these with you. If it is at all possible, I strongly encourage you to apply money directly towards your principal each month. Why, you might ask? Keep reading and I will show you.

I want you to try to make at least one extra mortgage payment every year. The easiest way to do this is to sign up to pay your mortgage bi-weekly. These bi-weekly payments will be half of what your monthly payments are but, since there are fifty-two weeks in a year, you will make twenty-six payments. Half of twenty-six is thirteen which is the number of full payments you will make each year using this approach. This is a plan that you can make happen automatically; just ask your mortgage lender how to do it. We are going to use the before mentioned $120,000 mortgage as our example. If you utilized this plan, you would pay off your mortgage seven years sooner and save approximately $41,000 on a thirty year loan! What if you want to pay off your loan even faster than this? Let's say you apply $100 each month towards your principal. You would save over $54,000 and pay this loan off in twenty years. As you can see, the more money you put towards the principal of your mortgage, the more you end up saving.

School Days

Tracy and I both got teaching jobs at schools located within five miles of our house. This got us thinking that maybe we could have just one car. Yes, I said one car! I know that may sound impossible to some of you, but we told ourselves that we would give it two months and re-evaluate. Two months passed and it seemed liked this would work. I dropped Tracy off at her school and went to my school. In the afternoon, I picked her up and we went home. It was actually nice spending our drive together talking about our days. There were some days that Tracy or I would have meetings or something else would come up and this routine would not work. On these occasions, we would arrange to catch rides with a co-worker or I would ride my bicycle to school—sometimes you just have to do whatever it takes.

After realizing that we could make it with one car, we sat down and came up with a way that would enable us to have it paid off by the time we were going to have a baby. We owed around $25,000 on the car loan so to have it paid off in two years, we would have to pay about $1,000 a month towards this loan. To see if this was possible, I made a list of our monthly expenses and deducted this from our salaries. Here is what this list looked liked:

Mortgage	$565
Roth IRA	$100 (more on this later)
Utilities	$44.00
Credit Card	$12.95 (for our internet use)
Student Loan	$203.79
Car Payment	$425.38
Phone Bill	$52.00
Satellite	$56.00
Life Insurance	$24.50
Electric Bill	$120.00
Total	$1,603.62

Our monthly salaries were $3,890.00 (after taxes) so we had $2,286.38 left over after paying our expenses. For me to be comfortable with Tracy staying home, I wanted to have $8,000 in our savings account. This amount would allow us to pay for our expenses and food for at least four months. Most financial advisors recommend you have an emergency account that contains enough money to cover three to six months of your living expenses. What if you lose your job or your car breaks down? With this money, you will be able to pay your bills until you are employed again and pay for any repairs without having to put these charges on a credit card. That meant we needed to save $275.00 each month (we already had $1,400 in our savings account). This left us with $2,011.38. Take $700 away from this amount for the extra car payment, and that left $1,311.38. We decided to keep our weekly spending money at $200, so that left us with around $500 for miscellaneous stuff ($200x4 weeks in a month = $800. $1,300-$800 = $500). It does seem incredible that we still had money left over, but we did. Even if our mortgage payment was $1,000 each month, we still would have been able to make extra car payments, put money in our savings account, and save for retirement. See, I told you that it can be done, even on a teacher's salary.

Another important step Tracy and I did at this time was to meet with a financial advisor. Our wonderful advisor, Ryan Van Buren, actually talked with us for no charge since we were members of the Union (check with your school district to see if this applies to you). Ryan asked us what our goals were and devised a plan to help us reach them. We decided to open both a Roth IRA and a 403b account.

Each month we put $100 into a Roth IRA. We arranged

for this amount to come out of our accounts automatically—because we used this approach, we knew that even if we spent all our money, we still saved some for retirement. In addition, we had $50 per check deducted into a 403b account. We were paid twice a month so that adds up to $100 each month deposited into our 403b account as well. The unique thing about a 403b account is the money is taken directly out of your pay *before* taxes. This means that instead of making $50 less per check, we were really only missing approximately $35 ($50 taxed at 30% = $15. $50 - $15 = $35). We invested $170 each month for our retirements. That is only $42.50 a week or $6.70 a day. That is equal to a cup of coffee and a muffin or lunch at a fast food restaurant. If you put this amount into a retirement account instead of a fast food place you will not only lose weight, but will have a nice little nest egg waiting for you. How much, you ask? If you invest $200 a month and earn a modest 7% interest each year on this amount, after thirty years you will have $243,994.20! Yes, you read that correctly. For less than the cost of two value meals at McDonald's every day, you could have almost $240,000 waiting for you when you retire. That doesn't sound too bad, huh? For more ways to see how you can save $6.70 or more a day, please read David Bach's book, "The Automatic Millionaire."

The Magic of Compound Interest
You might wonder how I came up with getting $240,000

from investing only $200 a month. This is possible through a wonderful concept known as compound interest.

Compound interest is defined as interest which is calculated not only on the initial principal but also the accumulated interest of prior periods.

Before I show you how compound interest works, I must tell about something called the "Rule of 72." This rule is a quick way to see how long it will take the money you invest to double. The way to determine this is to take 72 and divide it by the percentage of interest you are earning on your money. I will calculate a few examples for you. If you average a 5% return on your savings, you will double your money in 14.4 years (72 divided by 5 equals 14.4). If you average an 8% return on your money, you will double the amount you invest in 9 years (72 divided by 8 equals 9). Now it's your turn. Let's say you average a 10% return on your retirement account. How long will it take for this money to double? If you came up with 7.2 years you got it since 72 divided by 10 equals 7.2. Now I am going to show you exactly how this works.

To make this easy, we are going to pretend that you invest $100 and this investment averages a 9% return a year. Using the Rule of 72, this money will double in 8 years (72 divided by 9 equals 8). The chart below shows you how this works.

Year	Money Earned From Interest	Total Amount of Money
0	$0.00	$100.00
1	$9.00 (9% of $100.00)	$109.00
2	$9.81 (9% of $109.00)	$118.81
3	$10.69 (9% of $118.81)	$129.50
4	$11.66 (9% of $129.50)	$141.16
5	$12.70 (9% of $141.16)	$153.86
6	$13.85 (9% of $153.86)	$167.71
7	$15.09 (9% of $167.71)	$182.80
8	$16.45 (9% of $182.80)	$199.26

What an amazing concept! I bet you can now see how to turn $200 a month into $240,000. If you think about it, you would really be making almost four times your investment. You would have invested $72,000 (30 years times 12 months in a year equals 360. 360 times $200 a month equals $72,000) and gotten back $240,000. Even Albert Einstein had an opinion about compound interest. He once called it, "the greatest mathematical discovery of all time." This coming from the man that discovered the Theory of Relativity. Compound interest must be pretty powerful stuff, huh? I strongly encourage you to let compound interest begin to work it's magic for you.

What is a 403b and a Roth IRA

Some of you might not know what a Roth IRA or a 403b plan is so I am going to explain each to you.

A Roth IRA is named after its chief legislative sponsor, the late U.S. senator William Roth. IRA stands for individual retirement account. A Roth IRA is a tax-advantaged retirement account that allows you to make an after-tax contribution of up to $4,000 during the years 2005–2007 (this amount increases to $5,000 in 2008). For persons who are fifty or older, a special catch-up clause allows you to contribute an additional $500 a year. If you keep a Roth IRA for at least five years and are 59 and one-half years old or older when you begin to withdraw from this account, the entire account can be distributed tax-and penalty free. This is a great advantage if you are currently in a low tax bracket but expect to move into a higher tax bracket as you get older (which, since you are reading this book, I am sure you do). How does this help me, you ask? Let's say you are currently in the 20% tax bracket. If you invest $200 a month into a Roth IRA, you will pay $40 in taxes (20% of $200 is $40). Over the course of your working life this money will continue to grow. When you turn sixty, you decide to retire and start collecting this money. By now you are making more money and, thus, have moved up into the 40% tax bracket. Well, guess what? Since you have already been taxed on this money, you get to keep *all of it!* Even though you are now in the 40% tax bracket, you only had to pay half that amount in taxes. That sounds like a good plan to me.

There are some other advantages in opening a Roth IRA. Under certain conditions, up to $10,000 from this type of account may be withdrawn early to pay for a first home. If you have held the account for at least five years and become disabled, your entire balance may be distributed tax-and penalty-free. The greatest advantage in opening a Roth IRA may be its lack of forced distributions based on age. Most retirement plans require withdrawals to begin on April 1st of the calendar year after you reach the age of 70 and one-half and mandate an annual minimum distribution once withdrawals begin at any age beyond 59 and one-half. The Roth IRA does not require any of these.

A 403b account is a retirement savings plan offered to employees of tax-exempt organizations such as schools, churches, charities, and other not-for-profit groups. The contributions to these plans are made by employees, though in some cases the employer will match any donated funds.

Through payroll deductions, employees can contribute up to $15,000 annually into a 403b plan. The exception to this applies to employees over 50 years old. Such people can contribute an additional $5,000 annually. Both of these amounts will gradually increase in $500 increments in order to keep up with inflation.

The benefit of a 403b plan is the way your earnings grow. Since all contributions to this plan are made before income taxes are deducted, your earnings grow tax-deferred until you take a distribution. When you take a distribution, you will pay ordinary federal income tax on the taxable amount of your distribution. For more information on 403b retirement accounts, visit the website 403bwise.com.

Chapter 5

FEELING HOT, HOT, HOT

After the school year was over, Tracy and I analyzed our finances to see if we were on our way to meeting our goals. Summer is a great time for you teachers out there to do this since you have some time off. We had $5,800 in our savings account (a little more than we had expected), our car loan was being paid down and we were still able to travel. In November, we went to North Carolina for a friend's wedding. In December, we traveled to St. Augustine, Florida for a few days of relaxation. We were very busy that summer. We spent a week in New Orleans, a week in Ohio, and five days in Tennessee renting a cabin with family. We did all this and still met our financial goals.

Tracy and I did another important thing that year. We both signed up for disability insurance. This insurance is available to most of you. I do not plan on becoming disabled and I am sure you don't either, but life doesn't always play out the way we intend it to. The way my disability insurance worked was if I was injured for a certain amount of time and could not work, I would still collect 66% of my salary until I turned sixty-five. Not a bad safety net, huh? The amount of time you need to be disabled before collecting depends on the amount you pay into this plan—the less money you put in, the more time you have to wait. I signed up for a 90-day period. This means that if I were to become disabled and not able to work, I would still get paid approximately $1,600 every month after my 90-day wait period was over. I had to pay $28.80 a month for this coverage. This amount was taken out of my check before taxes, so I was really only missing about $20 each month. Not a bad deal, if I do say so myself. We did something a little different for Tracy. We knew that we were going to start trying to have a baby soon so we signed up for the option that best benefited us. There was a plan that would start paying once you spent the night at a hospital. When Tracy had the baby, she would have to spend a few nights in the hospital so this plan was the best choice for her. This option cost us $45.90 a month. Once again, this money was taken out before taxes so we really only missed around $32.00 each month. Although $32.00 is a decent amount of money, I will tell you later on how this turned out to benefit us greatly.

I have a cautionary note for you if you plan on signing up for disability insurance to help pay for your expenses after you have a baby. Make sure you obtain this insurance *before* you become pregnant. If you wait until you are pregnant, you might not qualify to receive money after having your baby because your pregnancy was a pre-existing condition. Tracy signed up in November and we had to wait until her coverage began in January before we started trying to get pregnant. I advise you to check into this before signing up for disability insurance since the rules and regulations vary depending on the company.

Another important step we took that summer was to analyze whether we were getting the most out of our savings. Like most people, we had a standard checking and savings account. We held these accounts at the same bank so it was easy to transfer funds between them. We were earning a little interest on the money we had in these accounts. I started doing some research and discovered money market savings accounts. These accounts are very similar to basic savings accounts except they earn more interest! At my bank, the interest earned on money market accounts is as follows:

Less than $2,500	0.55%
$2,500-$9,999	0.60%
$10,000-$24,999	1.49%
$25,000-$49,999	1.98%
$50,000-$99,999	2.18%

Although the interest earned on this account is not great, it sure beats nothing. If I put $10,000 in my money market account, I would have $10,149 at the end of the year. If I told you I would give you $149 for reading this book would you be happy to take it? I'm sure you would. If you think about it, a bank is paying you to place your money in one of their accounts. There are not many instances in which a bank will give you money so I would take full advantage of this opportunity.

There is a Cure for the Summer-Time Blues

Speaking of summers, if you are a teacher, you probably will not get "paid" during this time. What I mean by this is you will not get an actual paycheck throughout the summer months. In some counties, teachers receive twenty-four checks a year (they get paid on the 15th and 30th or 31st of each month). The last day of school is usually at the beginning of June and teachers receive five checks at this time—their pay for June 15, June 30, July 15, July 31, and August 15. The new school year begins in mid-August, so this means that teachers do not get paid until the end of August. You would not believe how many teachers have no money left from their summer pay once August rolls around. I have a way to guarantee this will not happen to you. As soon as you get your summer checks, deposit them into your money market savings account (if you do not have one of these accounts yet, I know you will open one soon since you now know the benefits of them). On the 15th and 30th of June, the 15th and 31st of July, and on August 15th, transfer the amount you normally get paid into your checking account. By using this approach, you are acting as your own employer. This method ensures that you do not blow your summer pay by the end of July and, thus, have to scramble in order to make it through August.

I know there are some school districts that pay their

employees only during the actual school year. If you fall into this category, I have a way for you to get "paid" during the summer too. Let's say you receive 18 pay checks throughout the school year. That leaves you 6 times to pay yourself during summer—24 (the number of times you would collect a check if you were paid twice a month) minus 18 equals 6. This means that you need to have enough money left over from your checks to pay yourself 6 times. I know you teachers out there can figure this out, but let's do an example for the fun of it.

We are going to say you earn $1,200 every two weeks after taxes are taken out. Take this amount and times it by 18, or the number of paychecks you receive in one year. This equals $21,600. Now take $21,600 and divide it by 24. This equals $900. The next step is to take the $1,200 you earn every two weeks and subtract $900 from it. The difference is $300. Every time you get paid, put $300 of your check into your savings account and, voila, you will never have to scrimp once the dog days of August roll around.

Let's face it, as teachers we know that the beginning of a school year is usually one of the most stressful times. Why not use my advice and eliminate one of these stresses from your life? Just think how nice it will be to have to only worry about getting ready for your students and not about how to scrape enough money together to pay for your groceries. I guarantee you that once you use this advice, you will wonder why you did not do it sooner.

Chapter 6

First Comes Love,
Next Comes Marriage,
Then Comes Baby in the Baby Carriage

In September of our second year home, we found out that Tracy was pregnant with the end of May being the due date. We were both very excited and prepared since we had been planning for this time.

On May 26th, 2004, our beautiful daughter, Ava Christelle, was born. As you parents out there know, nothing compares to becoming a father or mother. Even though we did not plan on the exact month we would have Ava, it turned out to be great timing. Tracy worked enough days to collect her summer pay and since it was summer, I was off work and able to help her out around the house.

The Pay-Off

Remember when I told you about obtaining disability insurance? Well, this is how it benefited us. In July, we started to receive the assorted bills for Ava's birth. Some of you may not know this, but even with health insurance, you will still have to pay some of your medical bills out of pocket. The hospital bill for Ava's birth totaled $2,318.50. That is a nice chunk of change, huh? I would not have wanted to pay that amount without planning for it first, since this would have reduced our savings to below our comfort level. After Tracy and Ava came home from the hospital, we had to have her doctor sign some papers and then we sent them off to our disability insurance company. Less than one month later we received a check from them in the amount of $2,293.33— almost enough to pay all of our hospital bills! Let's do the math to see how much we benefited by Tracy having disability insurance. We began paying for this coverage in November of 2002 and, remember, we really only missed approximately $32.00 a month. Next, we multiply 19 (the number of months Tracy had this insurance) times $32.00 and get $608. Take the difference of $2,293.33 and $608 and we ultimately made $1,685.33. Not only did we benefit financially by obtaining disability insurance, but we also had peace of mind knowing that we would receive a monthly payment if we ever became unable to work.

Like we do every summer, we went through our expenses to see if we were getting the most out of our hard-earned money. Looking through these, I discovered that we were paying way too much for our telephones—by now we were like most people and had a cell phone too. We had a premium package for our home phone service and were paying $52 each month for this plan. We were also paying $50 a month for our cell phone. Now, I may not be like some of you, but I hate the telephone. I feel like it is constantly ring-ing at my house and taking time away from me and my family. After going over our expenses, I realized we were spending over $100 every month on something we did not even like! Pretty stupid, if you ask me. I immediately changed our home phone plan to the basic package that cost $29 a month. I also cancelled our cell phone plan and purchased another one that allowed us to pay for only the minutes we used. This plan cost us around $10 each month. Just by taking thirty minutes and changing our phone plans, we saved $63 every month. That may not sound like too much, but that adds up to $756 a year. $756 goes a long way when you are trying to make it on one salary.

Our Plan Becomes Reality

Tracy and I had planned all along for her to stay home the entire first year of Ava's life. Before making this plan concrete, we did a little research and discovered a way that at least one of us would be home with Ava and enable us to save money. One of the greatest advantages of being a teacher (besides having summers off) is the benefits you get. In the county where we worked, not only do teachers have free health insurance, but if both spouses are teachers, their children's health insurance is free too! With the rising costs of health insurance, this is a huge benefit. Tracy and I originally planned to place her and Ava on my policy with the school district. The money for this policy would be deducted from each of my paychecks and would cost approximately $300 every month.

I do not know if you are aware of this, but in 1993 a federal law titled the Family Medical Leave Act was passed. This act provides an entitlement of up to twelve weeks of job-protected, unpaid leave during any 12-month period to eligible, covered employees for the following reasons:

- Birth and care of the eligible employee's child or placement for adoption or foster care of a child with the employee;
- Care of an immediate family member (spouse, child, parent) who has a serious health condition; or
- Care of the employee's own serious health condition.

This law requires that the employee's group health benefits must be maintained during this leave.

To be eligible for FMLA leave, an individual must meet the following conditions:

- Be employed by a covered employer and work at a worksite within 75 miles of which that employer employs at least 50 people;
- Have worked at least 12 months (these

months do not have to be consecutive) for the employer; and

- Have worked at least 1,250 hours during the 12 months immediately before the date FMLA leave begins.

What do you think we decided to do next? If you said Daddy Daycare, collect $200 and proceed directly to go.

Stay-At Home Dad

I know that some men probably think I am crazy for electing to stay home with a fairly new-born baby, but it would benefit us in several ways. First, I would get valuable bonding time with my daughter. I would also obtain a greater appreciation for stay-at-home moms (which Tracy would eventually become). Last, but not least, this plan would save us a good deal of moolah. As I mentioned earlier, our original plan of having Tracy stay home would cost us about $300 a month in health insurance. By utilizing the Family Medical Act, we ended up saving $1,450 by not having to pay health insurance for five months. This amount definitely made our plan worth it. I strongly encourage you to take advantage of this law because you will not only save money, but more importantly, you will get to spend irreplaceable time with your child.

Chapter 7

THE SUMMER OF HURRICANES

As many of you know, the summer of 2004 was a very busy time for we Floridians. The peninsula was hit with five hurricanes! The month of September was crazy for my family. Hurricane Frances struck on September 4th. My family evacuated across the state to get out of harm's way. Upon returning home, we were relieved to see that our house did not sustain any damage. In fact, we had gotten our electricity back by the time we got home. The rest of our family did not so some of them came and stayed with us. We had six additional people and three dogs living with us for one week. After everyone had gotten their electricity turned on and moved back home, our lives began to get back to normal. Then, one week later, another hurricane was barreling towards us.

Two days before Hurricane Jeanne was projected to hit, we evacuated to the west coast again. We stayed over there until a few days after Jeanne had passed and then began the trek home. We were not as fortunate this time. Our house needed a new roof, new carpet, and a few other repairs.

Finding the Silver Lining

The hurricanes were definitely a horrible experience that caused widespread damage throughout our city and state, but being the optimistic person that I am, I believe that behind every setback exists unforeseen opportunities.

Tracy's father was an insurance adjustor and decided to get back into this business after these storms. Tracy is very good with technology and he "hired" her to run his computer program and figure out insurance claims caused by the hurricanes.

As I mentioned earlier, our roof, porch and carpet were damaged and had to be replaced. Being a teacher, I had many contacts with parents of my students that could do these repairs. When all was said and done, we were able to do all of our repairs with the money we received from our insurance company. Now I would never wish for a hurricane or other natural disaster to strike, but I believe you should always try to make the best out of whatever faces you. Instead of harping on the negative aspects of a situation, try and find the silver lining. Sometimes the best opportunities for growth come from what may seem like the worst circumstances.

Opportunities to Make Money

There are many opportunities for teachers to make extra money. Even though Tracy and I were able to live off one salary, we explored other ways to supplement our income.

One way we did this was by having Tracy watch another child. The average cost of daycare where we lived was $35 a day. A teacher that Tracy worked with needed someone to watch her son every so often. Tracy did not have to take this on, but she decided a little extra money would not hurt, so she agreed to. She averaged watching Joshua four times a month which meant an additional $140 for us to put towards our monthly expenses.

I also decided to supplement our income by tutoring one of my students. I charged $50 an hour for my services. By this time, Tracy had told me that we were going on a trip the following September to celebrate my 30th birthday (she did not tell me where we were going). Since we did not need this additional money to cover our expenses, I decided to put it in an envelope and let it build. By the time September came, I had over $1,000 saved! We ended up going to New York City. I am glad to report that my tutoring money paid for some of our hotel and all our spending money. Putting this money in an envelope was not the smartest move financially speaking since it did not earn any interest, but I knew it was money that was going to be spent fairly soon so I just decided to hoard it. We had a great time in the Big Apple using money that did not come out of our paychecks.

If you want to live off one teacher's salary, there are other ways to increase your income. A lot of schools offer an after-school recreation program for their students. Working one of these programs may generate enough extra money to enable your spouse to stay home.

As I mentioned before, tutoring can be very lucrative. If you tutor twice a week for one hour, that could be an additional $100 in your pocket—that's $400 a month which would probably be enough to pay for health insurance for your spouse and child(ren).

You could also do as Tracy did and watch another child or two. Let's say you take in two children and charge $35 a day for watching each of them. This would give you $350 each week or $1,400 a month! That's not too bad, huh?

Another way for you teachers to earn extra money is to become nationally certified. This is an extremely long and challenging task, but it is well worth the effort. You will not only professionally benefit from this experience, but financially as well. Once you obtain this certification, you are eligible to receive an additional 20% of the median teacher's salary every year for up to ten years (the monetary awards for being nationally certified vary state to state so be sure to check with your county before pursuing this). Tracy obtained her certification in 1999 and it has helped us greatly.

As I mentioned, the manner in which you receive your monetary stipend varies state to state, but in our county, teachers got a check around Christmas. This check totals approximately $3,100. This money definitely comes in handy with the holidays approaching quickly. In addition, teachers can earn another $3,100 by mentoring other educators during the school year. The number of hours Tracy had to mentor was a little over 90 so this was not easy to obtain, but it was worth the time. In fact, Tracy and I used this money to pay for our health insurance premiums while she stayed home with Ava and, thus, did not have to take this amount out of my salary. The main idea I am trying to get across here is if you are serious about living off one salary, there are many opportunities out there that can help you achieve this goal.

Staying home might not cost as much as you think. Let's go over some of the expenses you would incur by working full-time. Day-care per week would average $125 (some places this figure will be more, others less). If you and your spouse both work you will probably eat out more than you would if one of you stayed home. I know of some families that are so exhausted by the end of the day they do not feel like cooking and eat out five times a week! We are going to say you eat out three times during the course of a week and the cost each time is $20. You would also have to use more gas driving to and from daycare so we'll add $25 a week for this expense. If you add all these child care related expenses you get $210 every week. I don't know how much your pay-check is but after taxes, I took home approximately $500 a week. Take $210 away from that and you get $290. Now all you have to do is figure out a way—I listed some earlier—to earn that amount each week. I know this is easier said than done, but if you are serious about living on one salary you can find a way to do it.

Chapter 8

A Summer of Change

Like we do every summer, we analyzed our finances to see how we were doing. It may sound amazing, but we had $7,000 in our savings—we had to use only $1,000 during the course of the school year when one of us stayed home.

Tracy and I had been working on a plan for the following school year. Tracy and another teacher presented their principal with the following proposal: Tracy would work 60% and Michele 40% of the school year. The way this would play out is Michele would work Mondays and Tuesdays with Tracy working Wednesdays, Thursdays, and Fridays. This plan would enable Tracy to stay home with Ava on Mondays and Tuesdays. Ava would spend Wednesdays with my grandparents, Thursday with a family friend, and Fridays with my mom. Since we now knew that we could live off my salary, we would be able to put the money Tracy earned into our savings account and start preparing for our next child. This plan allowed us to have the best of both worlds—Tracy would earn extra money and Ava would not have to be placed in a big daycare facility.

We also made a big purchase (for us at least) at the beginning of summer. We decided to become like most

Americans and have two cars. We would still only have one car payment and have extra money since Tracy was going back to work part-time. We bought a used mini-van with our monthly payments totaling $415. Tracy and I made it our goal to have this loan paid off in two years so that by the time we had another baby we would be without a car payment. We knew this was possible since we had already done it before with our first car.

During the summer I also decided to make a huge change—I was going to get out of teaching. I loved being a teacher but an opportunity was presented to me in which I could possibly double or even triple my salary. Tracy and I discussed the pros and cons of taking this risk and decided that I should give it a go. We were planning ahead and thought that this potential increase in salary would help us reach our goal of her staying home full-time faster than if I remained a teacher. It was an extremely difficult decision for me. I feel as though I was put on earth to teach and thought I was selling myself out for the almighty dollar. The more I pondered this, I realized that I was changing careers for the right reason—to better my family. I was slated to begin working at Florida Floor Fashions on August 1st which meant that I still had summer off and time to spend with my family.

Tracy and I also made one more important decision that summer. We had been talking for some time about putting an addition onto our house. We wanted to add an entire master suite. We asked around and it seemed like we could do this for $30,000. At this time, we owed $68,000 on our current mortgage so we were going to refinance for $100,000. After discussing this with Ryan (our financial advisor), we decided to refinance for $130,000. Why, you might ask? Well, we owed around $24,000 on our mini-van so we paid that loan off. We still owed $5,000 on Tracy's student loan so we paid that off as well. Our monthly mortgage payment increased by $350, but we no longer had a car or student loan payment. To some this move might not have made sense, but let me explain why we did it. Even though we were technically paying for the mini-van for thirty years, it will still benefit us. Our car loan had an 8% interest rate, whereas the mortgage rate was 6.65%. You can also write off mortgage interest on your income tax return. After paying off our car and student loans, we still had $30,000 set aside for our addition. At this point, we were not doing that bad. We had no debt, owned two cars outright, and had almost $40,000 in our money market account.

At this time we began to think about where we wanted to be in two years. I figured that if we saved most of Tracy's salary she would be able to stay home indefinitely after we had another baby. The plan was for her to work full-time during the 2006–07 school year. She would hopefully have the baby around March 2007 and, if all went according to plan, she would be able to stay home for as long as she wanted.

Another Move

Things were moving along smoothly after the summer of 2005. Tracy began school and liked working only three days a week. I was enjoying my new job selling flooring. It was difficult at first having to learn a lot of new information, but as time passed, I grew more and more comfortable. The addition was starting to come into place. We had the bedroom plans drawn, the truss plans were in the works, and we hired someone to build it. Then, October came.

Chapter 9

A Change of Plans

At the end of October, a hurricane hit us again. We thought we were in the clear since most hurricanes strike between July and September, but sure enough Wilma was heading our way. I had to take down all of our Halloween yard decorations and do what had now become an annual ritual—put up hurricane shutters. Wilma did not cause a lot of damage in our area compared to the previous two hurricanes but it did impact our day-to-day lives. Tracy, Ava, and I were without electricity for one week and moved in with friends until our power came back on.

A few weeks after Wilma passed, a teacher that worked with Tracy was diagnosed with cancer and told that she had only four months to live. This really got me thinking. I enjoyed my job but it was not as fulfilling for me as teaching was. At the end of the day I did not feel that I had done anything to make the world a better place. In my short time out of the classroom I realized that although teaching is an extremely difficult job, it made me a complete person. At this time I began to think about getting back into the teaching profession.

I also started thinking about any regrets that I may have

had in my life. What if I was told I had only four months left on earth? Would I have done anything differently? There was one thing that I know I would regret not doing. Tracy and I always talked about eventually moving to a place where we could experience four seasons and cooler weather. We had both lived in Florida for most of our lives and were ready for a change. I told her that if we were going to move now would be the time. We were not going to put $30,000 into our house and then move. There are so many people out there that say, "I wish I would have_____years ago." You can fill in the blank with moved, changed jobs, went on a trip, etc. Tracy and I did not want to be like this. We then asked our families if they would consider moving and most of them said yes. Now the only question was—Where should we move?

Taking That Midnight Train to Georgia

We went to upstate Georgia for a family vacation during the summer of 2005 and loved it. We wanted to move somewhere that did not have harsh winters, but where you would get a feel of all four seasons. We did some research and found that Georgia met these needs.

Now that we knew the state we wanted to move to the next step was to determine where in Georgia to live. We wanted to move to an area that had some things to do— restaurants, shops, etc. We decided to look in the Athens area. We began looking online at houses in this region and were pleasantly surprised at their cost. The housing market in Florida had skyrocketed since we bought our home. We bought our house in July of 2002 for $89,000 and had it appraised in July of 2005 for $200,000! Through our research we planned on purchasing a home in Georgia for between $125,000-$140,000. We owed approximately $130,000 on our current mortgage. If we sold our house for it's appraised value of $200,000 and bought a $140,000 home, how much could we put down? If you said $60,000, you are almost correct. Remember, we still had $30,000 set aside for the addition that was not done, so we could put $90,000 down! If we bought a $140,000 house we would only have a $50,000 loan to pay off. That is less than some people owe on their cars. This means that we could own both of our cars, have no debt, and owe only $50,000 on our house! Not too shabby. In addition, we could have the best of both worlds—Tracy would be able to stay home and I could get back into teaching.

This move could benefit us in other ways too. Let's say we accelerate our mortgage payments and pay off our house in 10 years. We would own all of our possessions. Now we could buy another house and rent it. Remember when I showed you how much money you waste by paying rent? The opposite is true when you are the one renting out the house.

Let's say you purchase a house for $125,000. You take out a 30-year mortgage at a 7% interest rate. Your monthly payments (minus taxes and insurance) would be in the ballpark of $830. You rent this same house for $1,000 a month. Using simple math, you would make $170 every month which equals $2,040 a year. Not a bad little profit, huh? Well, it gets even better. We are going to say you continue to rent this house for the duration of the loan. Just by doing this, you would make $61,200 ($2,040 x 30). After this mortgage is paid off, you decide to sell. I am going to underestimate this percentage, but for arguments sake, we are going to pretend the value of this house increased 1% each year. If this is the case, your rental is now worth $170,000. If you sell it for this amount and add the $61,000 you made from renting you will have made $230,000 from nothing! Since you borrowed the money to buy the house from the bank and your renters paid the mortgage, the bank and renters made a lot of money for you. You should definitely send them both a nice Thank You card for treating you so well.

Chapter 10

Another Stroke of Good Fortune

In January of 2006, Tracy and some of my family took a long weekend trip to Georgia in search of houses. They spent most of their time in the Athens region and decided that was where we should move.

Upon her return home, Tracy and I decided to put our house up for sale. We were running the risk of selling it early and then having to live with someone for a few months (we were committed to our jobs until June), but if we waited until April or May to put it on the market it could have taken a few months to sell. We could not afford paying two mortgages so we put it up for sale in mid-January.

Our realtor, Kelly, came to our house on a Saturday morning at 9:00. We discussed all the items that go with selling a house and, by 10:30, we had a For Sale sign in our front yard. Fifteen minutes later Kelly called and said someone wanted to look at our house. She asked if we would show it because she was too far away. We did and the woman seemed to like it. An hour later Kelly phoned again and said the woman wanted to come back with her husband. We said no problem and showed our home to the two of them. The husband seemed pleased with what he saw and said they would be contacting Kelly. I thought this was a great start to our selling process—an interested customer in less than two hours.

Another hour passed when Kelly called yet again. She said there was someone else that wanted to view our house! We were fine with showing it again so in they came. This couple looked around for ten minutes before going out back. After conversing with each other for a few minutes they told me they wanted to make us an offer. I asked her to call Kelly with it so off they went. Tracy and I were in a state of shock! We had not even gotten used to the idea of actually putting our house up for sale and now it looked like it was sold.

Kelly called us and could not believe it herself. The couple offered $4,900 less than our asking price. I told Kelly that since our house had been for sale for less than four hours and we already had two sets of people interested in it I thought we should get as close to our asking price as we could. We countered with an amount $900 less than our asking price. The couple agreed without hesitation and so you have it—we sold our house in four hours for $199,000! We bought it for $89,000, so in three and one-half years, we made a nice little profit of around $100,000 after paying Kelly's commission.

Just think what we would have made if we rented rather than bought a house—nothing. Now we can buy a $140,000 house in Georgia and it will really be like purchasing a home for $40,000 since we can put $100,000 down. It was hard to move from this wonderful little house, but it enabled us to continue achieving our goals.

I know that moving is not possible for everyone. The main point I am trying to make is how important it is to own, rather than rent, your home. There might be a time in the future that you decide it is time to move. If you own your home you will get something in return for all those monthly mortgage payments you made.

Chapter 11

HELP, I AM KNEE-DEEP IN DEBT AND CAN'T GET OUT

I know most people did not have the same financial circumstances as I did. Most of you did not live the first two years of your marriage saving money without having any bills to pay, and I am most certain that none of you have a Bank of Meno, as I believe there is only one in existence. This chapter was written for those of you who are up to your eyeballs in debt and do not know what to do. I am going to give you advice on how to get yourself out of it but, I must warn you, it is not going to be easy.

We are going to say you have a mortgage, two car payments, a student loan payment, and owe $7,000 on one credit card and $4,000 on another. You are living paycheck to paycheck and have no money left over to do anything, let alone invest for your retirement. You are extremely stressed out and do not see how you are going to get out of this hole. I am going to show you how you can get rid of this debt. Like I mentioned earlier, this will not be easy but, with patience and sacrifice, you can pay off all your debt and rest peacefully at night knowing you no longer owe credit card companies anything.

The first action you need to take is to lock all of your credit cards in a safe (or put them somewhere out of sight so you will not use them). I know living life without any credit cards will be difficult for some of you, but this needs to be done if you are serious about getting out of debt.

The next step is to write down everything you spend for one month. This includes your car payments and grocery bills along with that morning coffee from Starbucks. After the month is up, review your list and see if there is anything you can do without. I know eliminating some of the things that bring you joy in life is not very fun but it is a necessary evil on your long road to obtaining financial freedom. We are going to say that you find a way to trim $200 from your monthly expenses. Now, you ask, what should I do next?

The most important goal you should have is to pay off your credit card debt. I am going to show you how much money you are spending on these two cards. We will start with the card that carries a $4,000 balance. Let's say the interest rate on this card is 18% and your monthly minimum payments are 2% of this balance. If you paid just this amount every month, it would take 508 months to get rid of this debt and cost you almost $11,000 in interest! Now, let's take the card with $7,000 on it and apply the same rates as listed above. Your monthly minimum payments would be $140 and it would take 620 months to pay-off the balance on this credit card. In addition, you will have paid over $20,000 by the time this loan is paid off. Between these two loans totaling $11,000 you will pay almost $31,000 in interest—that is around three times the original amount! We are going to see if we can lessen the pain a little bit.

If you remember, you discovered a way to trim your monthly expenses by $200. We are going to put this $200 to good use. I suggest you take half this amount and put it into a retirement account and use the other half to pay-off your debt. You might wonder why you should not use all of this money to pay down your debt. Since you do not have any money saved for your retirement as of yet and you do not want to work forever, you need to get started. I know you might not think $100 a month will enable you to save much, but let's do the math anyway. If you put $100 into a retirement account every month for twenty-five years and this money earns a modest 7% a year, guess how much you will have? How does $81,000 sound? That may not be a lot, but it sure beats nothing.

Using the remaining $100, you are going to pay-off your credit cards. You are going to apply this extra money towards the card that has least amount on it first. In this case, it is the $4,000 card. By paying an extra $100 a month on this card you will pay this balance off in 28 months and only $902 would go towards interest. This will enable you to pay this loan off 40 years earlier than you would by just making the minimum payments. You would also save almost $9,000! That does not sound too bad now does it?

After this first credit card is paid off you will start paying off the other one. If you apply $100 extra every month towards this loan, instead of just making the minimum monthly payments, you will pay it off almost 48 years earlier and save around $17,000. By using this approach, your credit card debt will be gone in approximately 6 years and you will have saved almost $26,000! Think how nice it will be to become debt-free and still have money set aside for your retirement. I bet you feel much better now than you did before reading this chapter. Now, the only thing left for you to do is be like Nike and "Just Do It."

Conclusion

If you become financially independent, you will have the freedom to pursue whatever you want. If you do not like your job, you will have the security to try something new. If you become bored with where you live, you can leave. The possibilities that will exist for you are endless.

I firmly believe that sometimes less can equal more. What I mean by this is having fewer possessions and things to worry about means you have more time to spend doing the things you really want to do—hang out with family and friends, walk in the park, read, travel, etc.

Think about your job for a moment. What if you did not depend on your paycheck to survive? If you had enough money in savings to cover your living expenses for awhile would that change the way you view your job? Think about all those things you voluntarily do. These might include playing with your children, exercising, or volunteering your services somewhere. I bet you have a different attitude about these tasks than you do your job. It works this way for most things in life. If you *have* to do something it often times becomes unfulfilling. The decision is up to you. Do you want to work to live or live to work?

In this book I have given you a sure fire way to live life to its fullest on a relatively low-scale salary. I know some of the steps my family and I took may seem improbable, but I hope you see that they can be done. At times we had to make sacrifices and not always get what we wanted but in the long run, these sacrifices have been well worth it.

I hope that you have gained valuable insight from this book. I know that not everything in it will directly apply to you, but I hope you are able to use some of my advice to enrich your life. Thank you for taking your precious time to read my story. I wish you the best of luck in all of your endeavors.

Epilogue

Since completing this book, a lot of good fortune has befallen my family. I ended up getting back into teaching at the beginning of March. A position teaching Autistic children opened up at Tracy's school and I was offered this job. I talked to my boss at Florida Floor Fashions and he gave me his blessings to go ahead and pursue this opportunity. I was extremely grateful for this and loved being a teacher again.

At the start of April, Tracy, Ava, and I ventured to Georgia to buy a house (we had been living with my parents since selling our house in February). We did some research on the internet and had a few houses that we wanted to look at. We fell in love with the first house we saw and made an offer. The seller agreed and we closed on it at the end of April.

Tracy and I drove back to Georgia for the closing and we had another stroke of good luck. We had heard through a friend that there was a job teaching special education students opening at a local elementary school. I really enjoyed teaching Autistic children so I decided to stop by the school and see if I could drop off my resume. The principal, Alisa Hanley, was very kind and made time to talk with me. She told me that she had someone else to interview and would be in contact with me. The next day Tracy and I drove back to Florida and Mrs. Hanley called and offered me the job. This definitely took a lot of stress off me—I knew that I could enjoy the rest of my time in Florida knowing that I had another job lined up.

Tracy, Ava, and I have loved living in Georgia. Fall is just beginning and the weather is wonderful. The greatest time of the day for me is leaving for work. I love spending time at home with Tracy and Ava, but it gives me great joy knowing that they get to stay home and spend everyday together. I sometimes sit back and think, "Wow, we did all this on a teacher's salary."

Danny Kofke October 2006

Appendix

Cystic Fibrosis is a chronic, progressive disease that causes mucus to become thick, dry, and sticky. The mucus builds up and clogs passages in many of the body's organs, but primarily in the lungs and pancreas. In the lungs, the mucus can cause serious breathing problems and malnutrition which can lead to growth and developmental problems. Cystic Fibrosis is usually diagnosed during childhood. At the moment, the life expectancy for someone with CF is around thirty-two years, but new treatments are increasing this. In fact, I must thank you because, by purchasing this book, you are helping find a cure for this awful disease since a portion of the proceeds go to the Cystic Fibrosis Foundation.

Bibliography

Bach, David. *Smart Women Finish Rich*. New York: Broadway Books, 1999.

Bach, David. *Smart Couples Finish Rich*. New York: Broadway Books, 2001.

Bach, David. *The Automatic Millionaire*. New York: Broadway Books, 2003.

Bach, David. *Start Late, Finish Rich*. New York: Broadway Books, 2005.

Bach, David. *The Automatic Millionaire Homeowner*. New York: Broadway Books, 2006.